EXPLORER PASSPORT

Number:
0123456789

Name: ______________________________

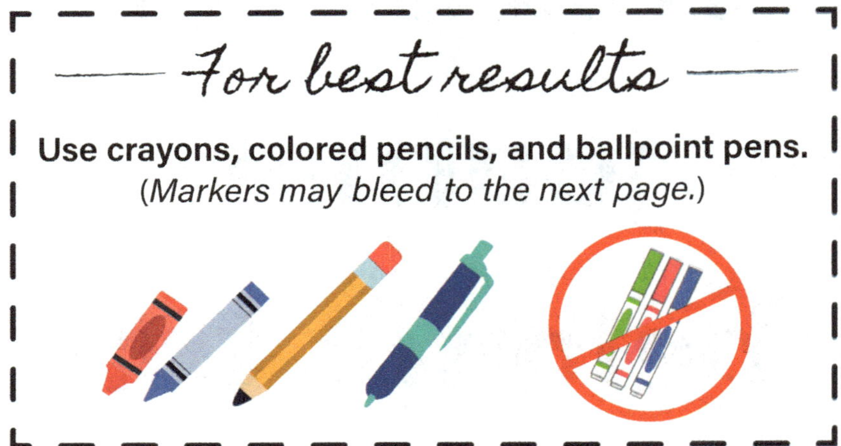

Book Title: My Adventures: A Kid's Travel Journal

ISBN/EAN: 978-90-828545-5-8

For more information, visit www.kibatales.com.

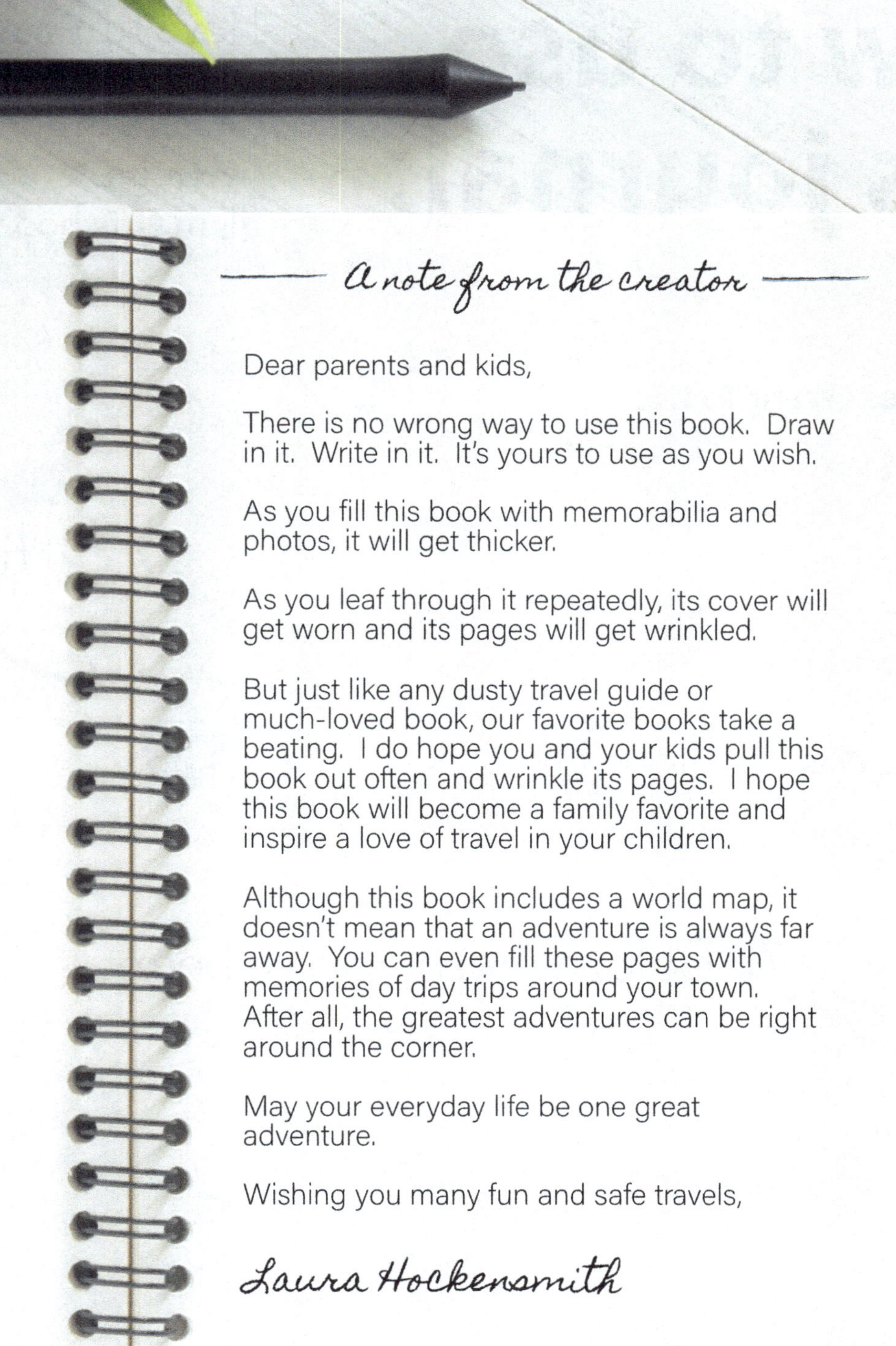

a note from the creator

Dear parents and kids,

There is no wrong way to use this book. Draw in it. Write in it. It's yours to use as you wish.

As you fill this book with memorabilia and photos, it will get thicker.

As you leaf through it repeatedly, its cover will get worn and its pages will get wrinkled.

But just like any dusty travel guide or much-loved book, our favorite books take a beating. I do hope you and your kids pull this book out often and wrinkle its pages. I hope this book will become a family favorite and inspire a love of travel in your children.

Although this book includes a world map, it doesn't mean that an adventure is always far away. You can even fill these pages with memories of day trips around your town. After all, the greatest adventures can be right around the corner.

May your everyday life be one great adventure.

Wishing you many fun and safe travels,

Laura Hockensmith

How to use this journal:

Have fun with it!

There is no wrong way to fill in this book.

It's yours!

1 Plan your future travels.

2 Color where you've been.

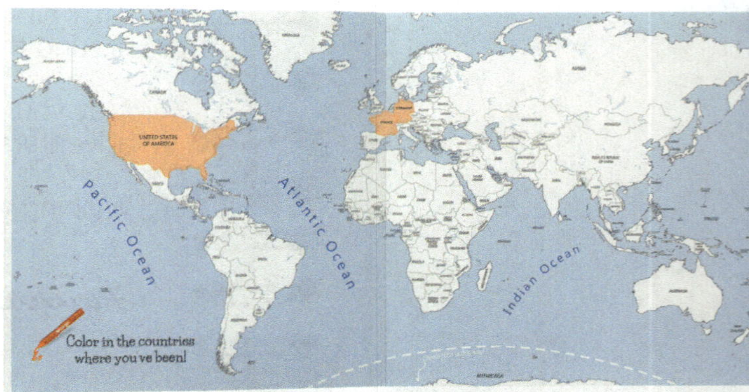

3 Track each trip over two-page spreads:

Write the details of the trip and your favorite memories.

Draw a picture.

Tape in memorabilia and photos.

Travel Preparation: Lists & Maps

Places I Want To Go:

- [ ]
- [ ]
- [ ]
- [ ]
- [ ]
- [ ]
- [ ]

GREENLAND
ALASKA (U.S.A.)
CANADA
UNITED STATES
OF AMERICA
Atlantic Ocean
Pacific Ocean
MEXICO
HAWAII (U.S.A.)
BAHAMAS
CUBA
HAITI
JAMAICA
BELIZE
GUATE-
MALA
HONDURAS
EL SALVADOR
NICA-
RAGUA
COSTA
RICA
PANAMA
VENEZUELA
GUYANA
SURI-
NAME
FRENCH
GUIANA
COLOMBIA
ECUA-
DOR
PERU
BRAZIL
BOLIVIA
CHILE
PARAGUAY
URU-
GUAY
ARGENTINA
MARSHALL
ISLANDS
NAURU
KIRIBATI
SOLOMON
ISLANDS
TUVALU
VANUATU
FIJI
SAMOA
NIUE
TONGA
COOK
ISLANDS
FRENCH
POLINESIA
PITCAIRN
ISLANDS
NEW
CALEDONIA
NEW
ZEALAND
Orange
Color in the countries
where you've been!

ICELAND
NORWAY
SWEDEN
FINLAND
ESTONIA
LATVIA
LITHUANIA
BELARUS
IRELAND
UNITED KINGDOM
GERMANY
POLAND
UKRAINE
CZECHIA
SLOVAKIA
AUSTRIA
HUNGARY
ROMANIA
FRANCE
ITALY
CROATIA
BOSNIA
SERBIA
BULGARIA
SPAIN
PORTUGAL
RUSSIA
KAZAKHSTAN
MONGOLIA
GEORGIA
UZBEKISTAN
KYRGYZSTAN
TURKMENISTAN
TAJIKISTAN
TURKEY
N. KOREA
S. KOREA
JAPAN
SYRIA
IRAQ
IRAN
AFGHANISTAN
PEOPLE'S REPUBLIC OF CHINA
LEBANON
ISRAEL
JORDAN
MOROCCO
TUNISIA
ALGERIA
LIBYA
EGYPT
SAUDI ARABIA
PAKISTAN
NEPAL
BHUTAN
INDIA
BANGLADESH
QATAR
U.A.E.
OMAN
TAIWAN
MYANMAR
LAOS
THAILAND
VIETNAM
CAMBODIA
NORTHERN MARIANA
MAURITANIA
MALI
NIGER
CHAD
SUDAN
ERITREA
YEMEN
DJIBOUTI
GUINEA
BURKINA FASO
NIGERIA
GHANA
CÔTE D'IVOIRE
LIBERIA
ETHIOPIA
CENTRAL AFRICAN REPUBLIC
SOUTH SUDAN
CAMEROON
SRI LANKA
PHILIPPINES
GUAM
FEDERAL STATES OF MICRONESIA
PALAU
MALAYSIA
MALDIVES
SOMALIA
UGANDA
KENYA
EQUATORIAL GUINEA
SÃO TOMÉ AND PRINCIPE
GABON
REPUBLIC OF THE CONGO
DEMOCRATIC REPUBLIC OF THE CONGO
RWANDA
BURUNDI
SINGAPORE
INDONESIA
SEYCHELLES
TANZANIA
PAPUA NEW GUINEA
TIMOR-LESTE
Indian Ocean
ANGOLA
ZAMBIA
MALAWI
MOZAMBIQUE
MADAGASCAR
ZIMBABWE
NAMIBIA
BOTSWANA
ESWATINI
LESOTHO
SOUTH AFRICA
AUSTRALIA
Antarctica is this way!
ANTARCTICA

Alaska
It's this way!
Alaska is much bigger than this!
Washington
Oregon
Idaho
Montana
Wyoming
Nevada
Utah
Colorado
California
Arizona
New
Mexico
Hawaii is much smaller than this!
It's this way!
Hawaii
MEXICO

CANADA
N. Dakota
Minnesota
Wisconsin
Michigan
Vermont
Maine
New Hampshire
Massachusetts
New York
Rhode Island
Connecticut
S. Dakota
Nebraska
Iowa
Illinois
Indiana
Ohio
Pennsylvania
New Jersey
Mary-land
Delaware
West Virginia
Virginia
Washington D.C.
Kansas
Missouri
Kentucky
North Carolina
Tennessee
Oklahoma
Arkansas
South Carolina
Missis-sippi
Alabama
Georgia
Texas
Louisiana
Florida
Orange
Color in the U.S. states where you've been!

Free Travel Resources!

PACKING List FOR KIDS!

Fill in the amou of each item your child needs to

Fill in additional things to pack in the blank spaces.

Have your child check the boxes as they gather each thing.

Orange

SUMMER

☐	Shirts ____	☐	Swim Suit
☐	Pants ____	☐	Hat
☐	Shorts ____	☐	Sunglasses
☐	Long Sleeve Shirts ____	☐	Water Bottle
☐	Sweatshirt ____	☐	Activities
☐	Rain Jacket ____	☐	Stuffed Animal or Blanket
☐	Socks ____	☐	
☐	Underwear ____	☐	
☐	Pajamas ____	☐	
☐	Shoes ____	☐	

INSPIRING LITTLE TRAVELERS

Kiba Tales Book Series: www.kibatales.com

Packing lists with pictures that teach kids to pack their own suitcase

Free Printable Activity Pages

for your next trip

Download them at

www.kibatales.com

My Trips

Antarctica
Excursion

AUSTRALIA
ARRIVAL

Atlantic Ocean Crossing
Plymouth
United Kingdom

PANAMA CANAL

DEPARTURE
MARRAKESH,
MOROCCO

JUNIOR
RANGER
ACADIA NP

Beijing

France Airport
Paris

How did you get there?

- [ ] Car
- [ ] Boat
- [ ] Bus
- [ ] Airplane
- [ ] Camper
- [ ] Train
- [ ] Bicycle
- [ ] Walking
- [ ] Hot Air Balloon!

- [ ] Sunny

- [ ] Sun & Clouds

- [ ] Cloudy

- [ ] Rainy

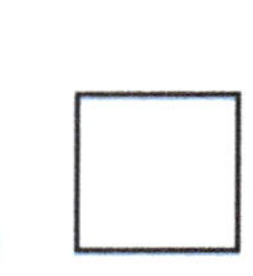

- [ ] Snow

With whom did you go?

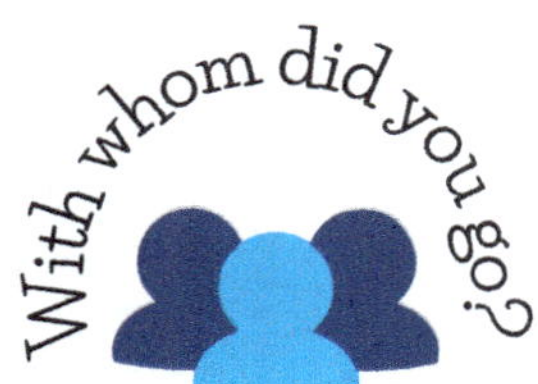

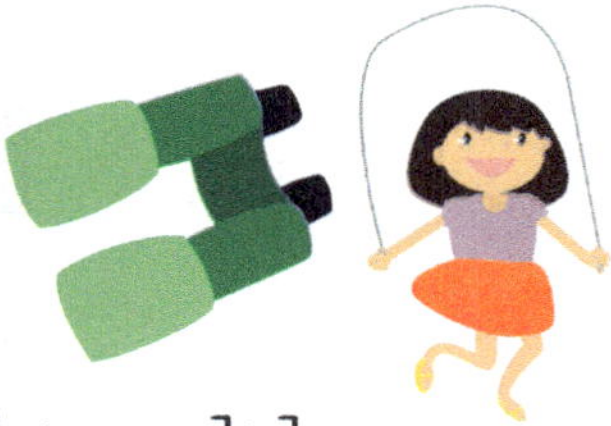

What things did you see or do?

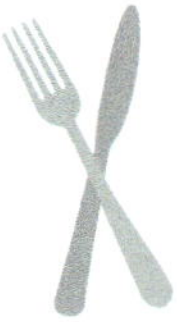

What did you eat?

What was your favorite part?

Draw a picture of something you saw:

Describe your drawing: ____________________

____

Glue or tape things from your trip here:

When?

____

How did you get there?

☐ Car ☐ Boat ☐ Bus

☐ Airplane ☐ Camper ☐ Train

☐ Bicycle ☐ Walking ☐ Hot Air Balloon!

How was the weather?

☐ Sunny

☐ Sun & Clouds

☐ Cloudy

☐ Rainy

☐ Snow

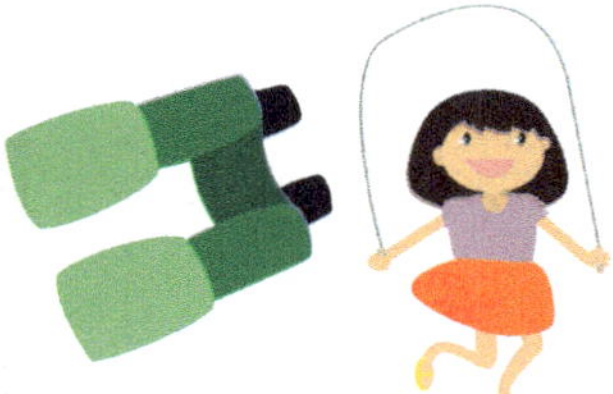

What things did you see or do?

What did you eat?

What was your favorite part?

Draw a picture of something you saw:

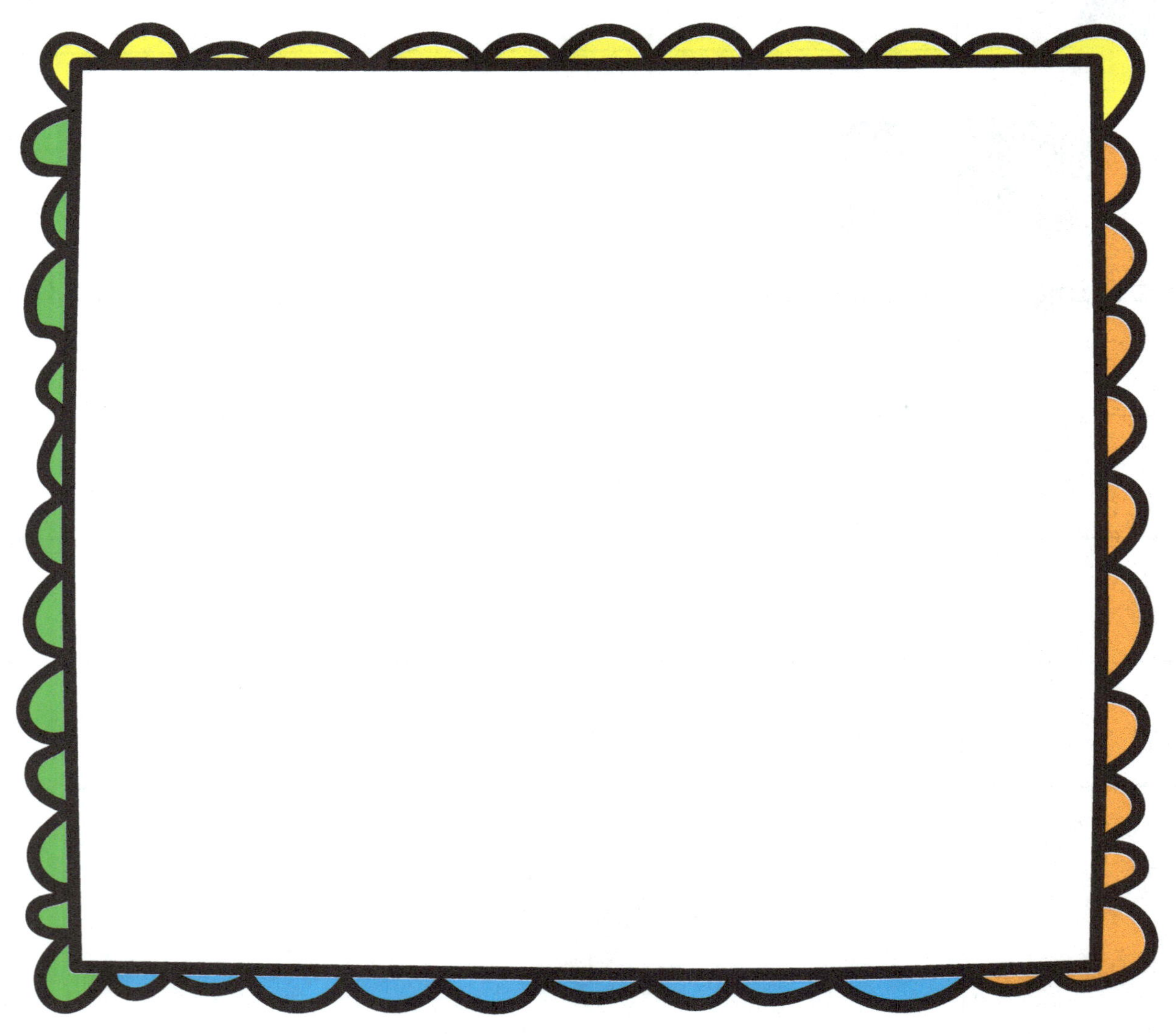

Describe your drawing: ______________________________

____

Glue or tape things from your trip here:

When?

____

How did you get there?

☐ Car ☐ Boat ☐ Bus

☐ Airplane ☐ Camper ☐ Train

☐ Bicycle ☐ Walking ☐ Hot Air Balloon!

How was the weather?

☐ Sunny  ☐ Sun & Clouds   ☐ Cloudy  ☐ Rainy 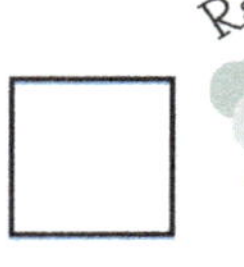  ☐ Snow 

With whom did you go?

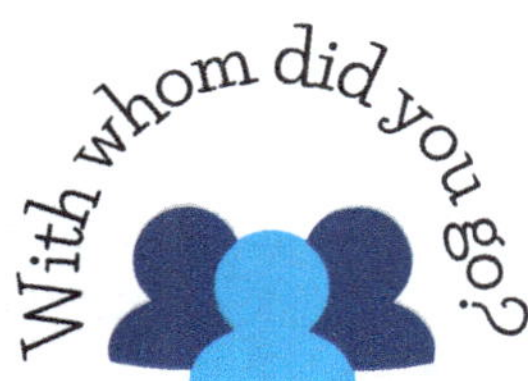

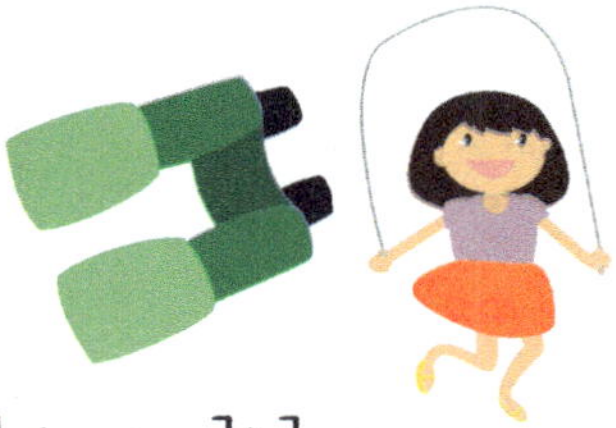

What things did you see or do?

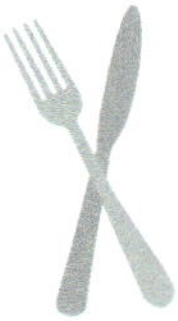

What did you eat?

What was your favorite part?

Draw a picture of something you saw:

Describe your drawing: ______________________

____

Glue or tape things from your trip here:

When?

How did you get there?

- [ ] Car
- [ ] Boat
- [ ] Bus
- [ ] Airplane
- [ ] Camper
- [ ] Train
- [ ] Bicycle
- [ ] Walking
- [ ] Hot Air Balloon!

How was the weather?

- [ ] Sunny

- [ ] Sun & Clouds

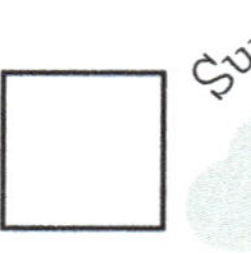

- [ ] Cloudy

- [ ] Rainy

- [ ] Snow

With whom did you go?

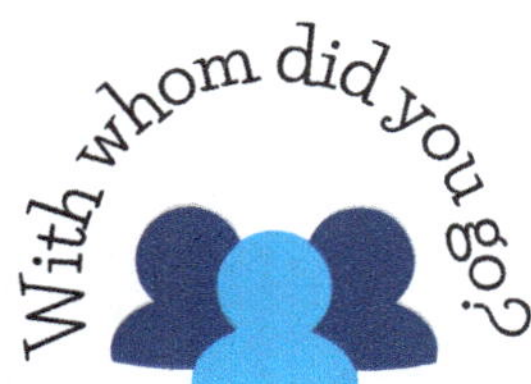

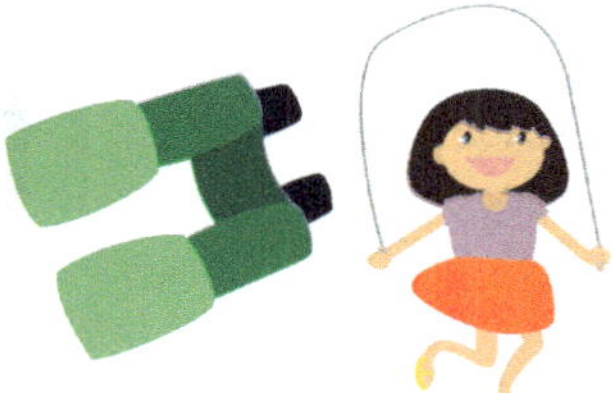

What things did you see or do?

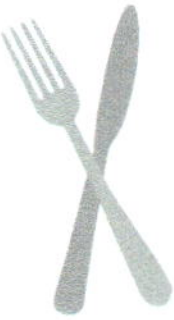

What did you eat?

What was your favorite part?

Draw a picture of something you saw:

Describe your drawing: ______________________________

____

Glue or tape things from your trip here:

How did you get there?

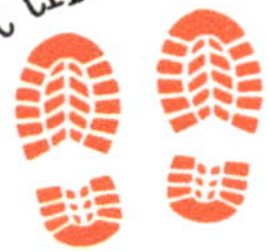

☐ Car

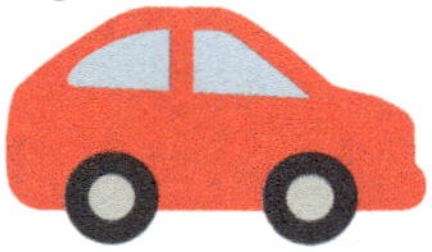

☐ Boat

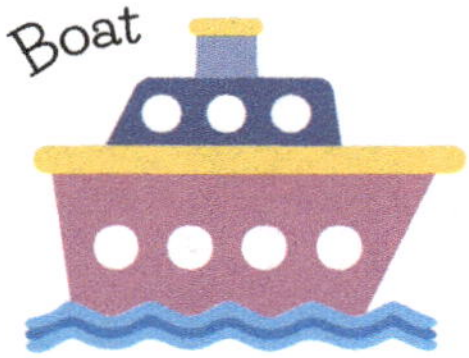

☐ Bus

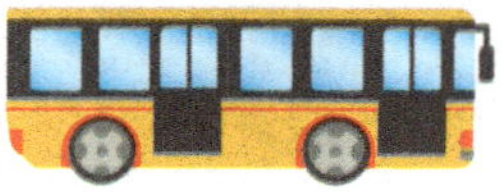

☐ Airplane

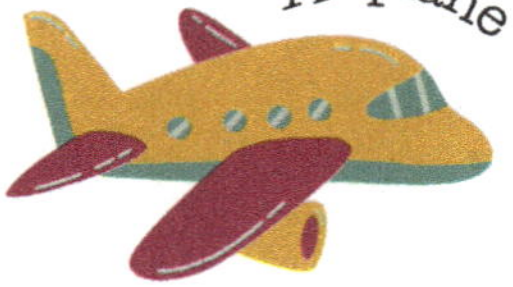

☐ Camper

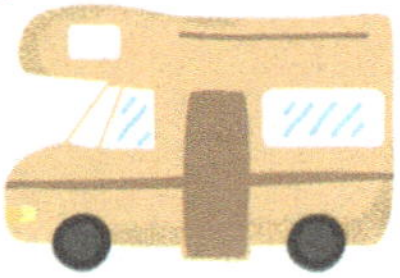

☐ Train

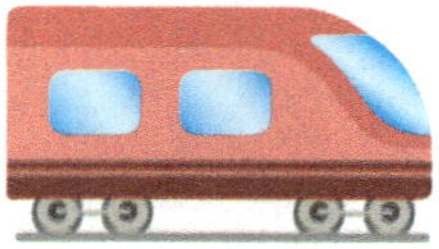

☐ Bicycle

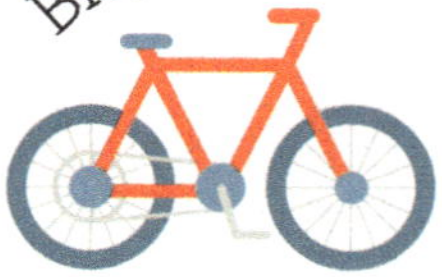

☐ Walking

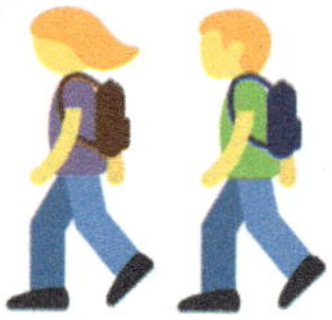

☐ Hot Air Balloon!

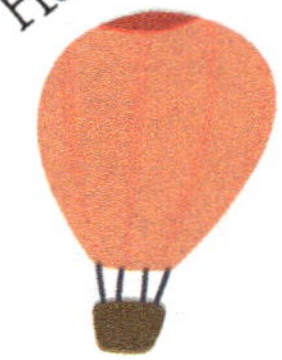

☐ Sunny

☐ Sun & Clouds

☐ Cloudy

☐ Rainy

Snow

With whom did you go?

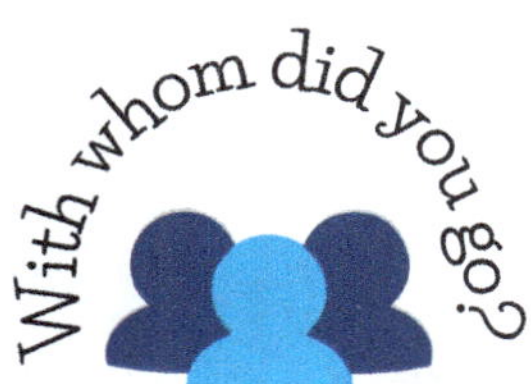

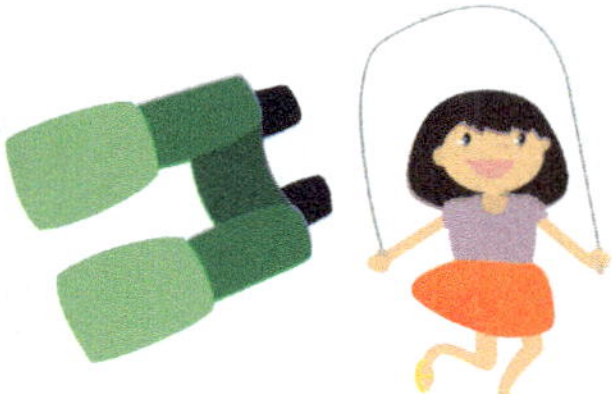

What things did you see or do?

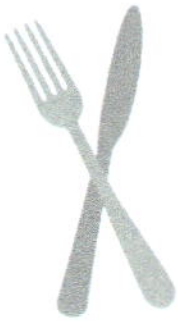

What did you eat?

What was your favorite part?

Draw a picture of something you saw:

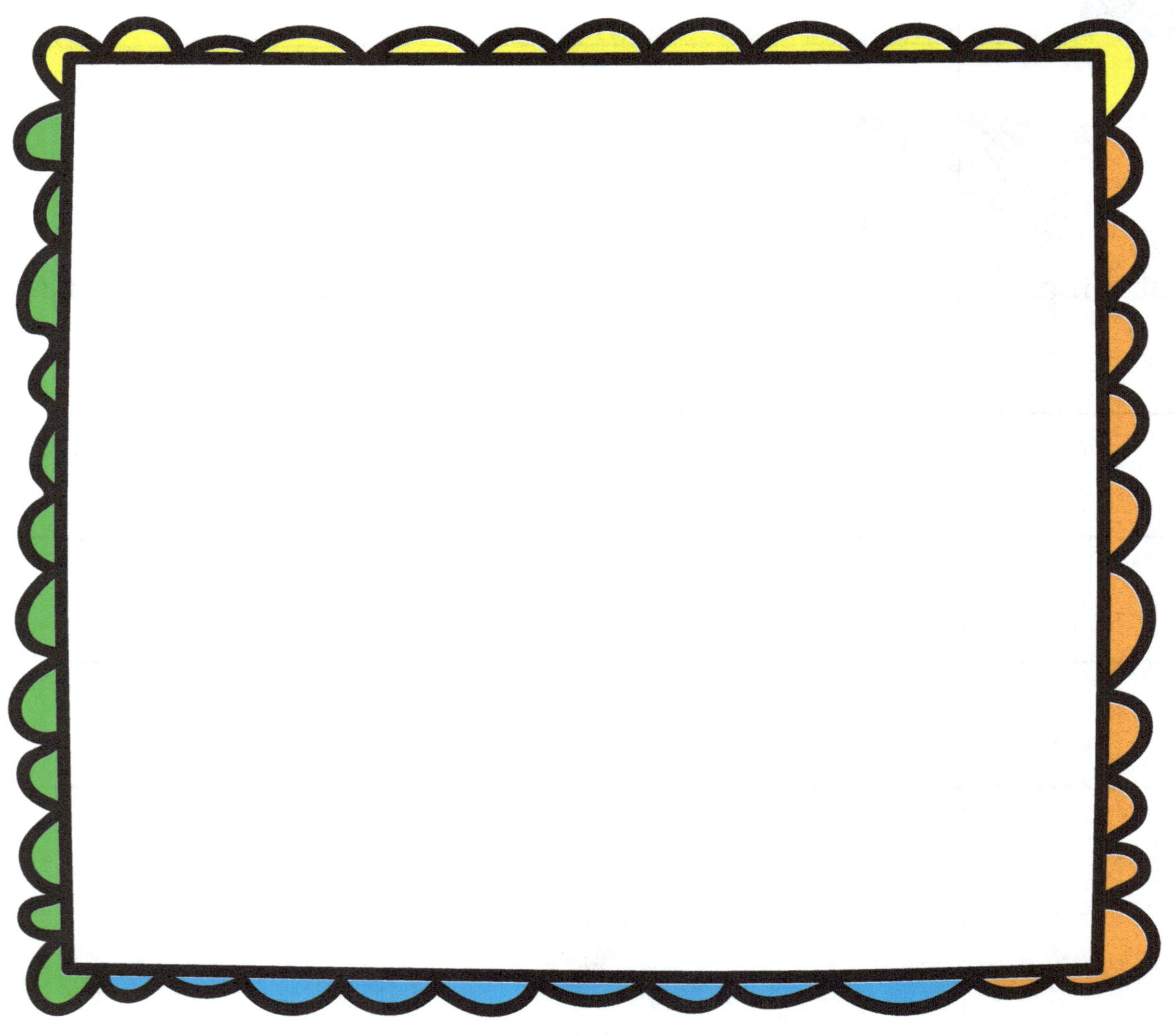

Describe your drawing: ______________________________

____

Glue or tape things from your trip here:

When?

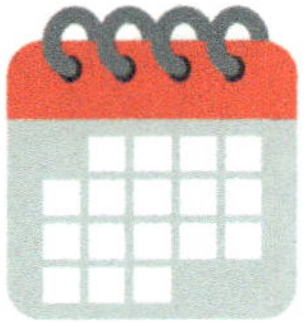

How did you get there?

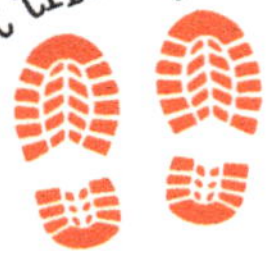

☐ Car 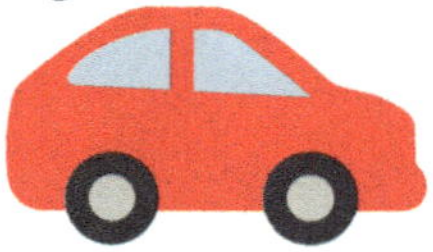 ☐ Boat 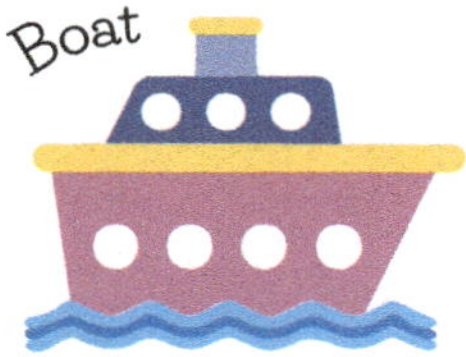 ☐ Bus

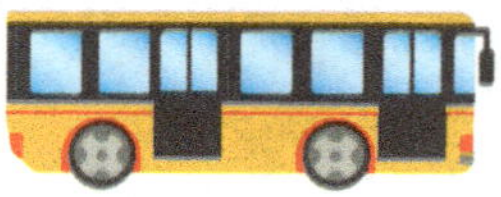

☐ Airplane 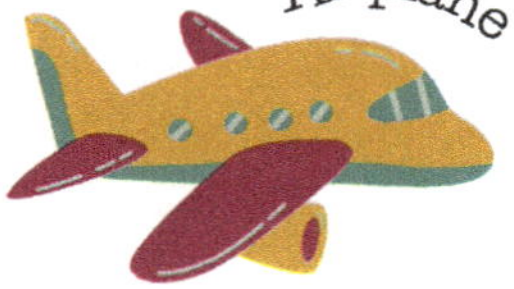 ☐ Camper 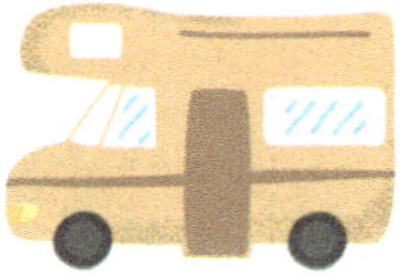 ☐ Train

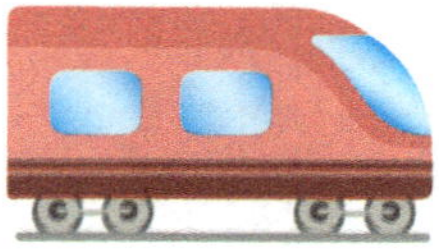

☐ Bicycle 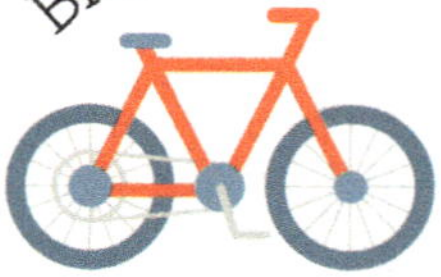 ☐ Walking 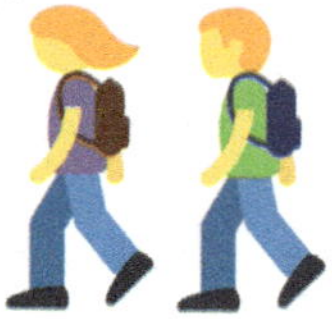 ☐ Hot Air Balloon!

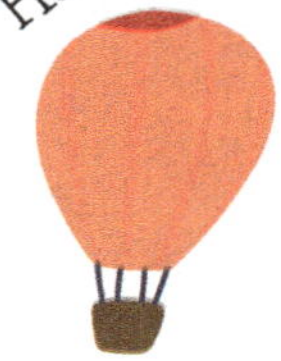

How was the weather?

☐ Sunny

☐ Sun & Clouds

☐ Cloudy

☐ Rainy

☐ Snow

With whom did you go?

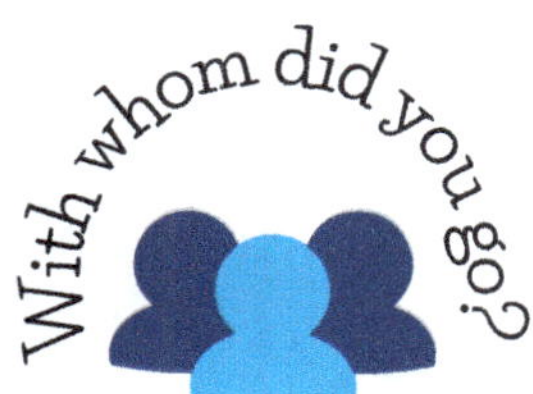

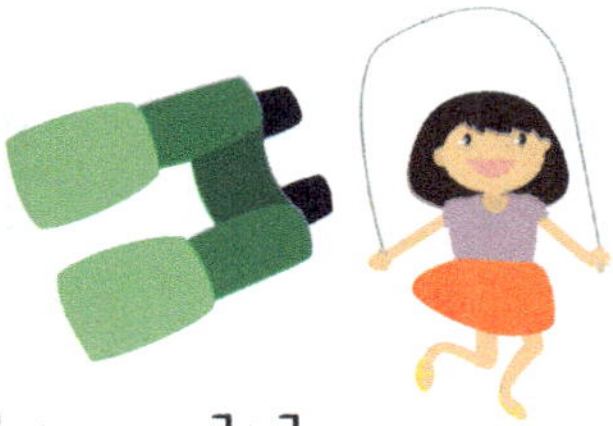

What things did you see or do?

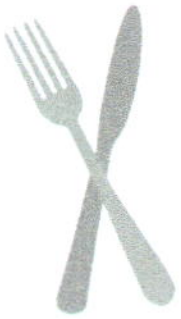

What did you eat?

What was your favorite part?

Draw a picture of something you saw:

Describe your drawing: ______________________________

____

Glue or tape things from your trip here:

When?

How did you get there?

☐ Car ☐ Boat ☐ Bus

☐ Airplane ☐ Camper ☐ Train

☐ Bicycle ☐ Walking ☐ Hot Air Balloon!

How was the weather?

Sunny

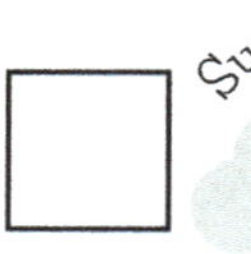

Sun & Clouds

Cloudy

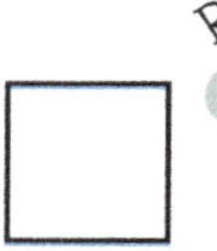

Rainy

Snow

With whom did you go?

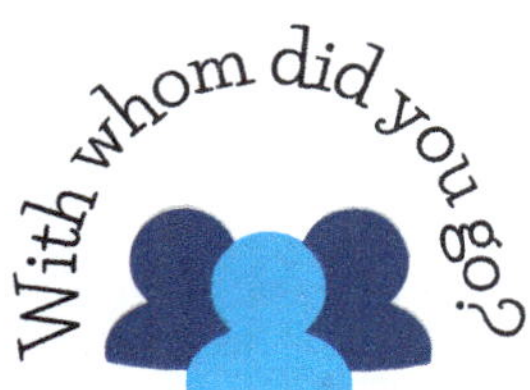

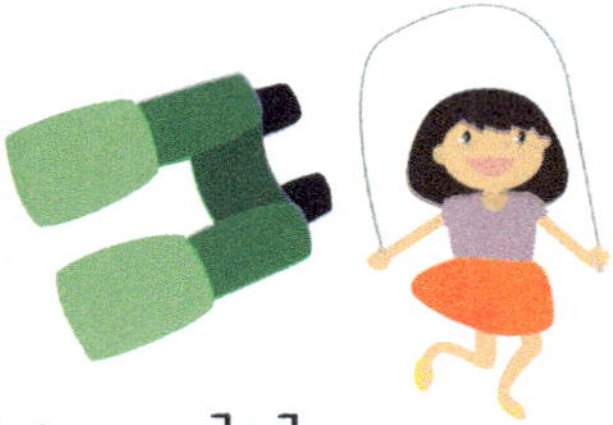

What things did you see or do?

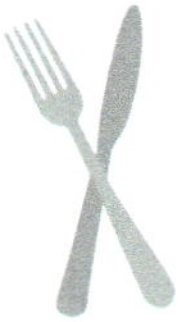

What did you eat?

What was your favorite part?

Draw a picture of something you saw:

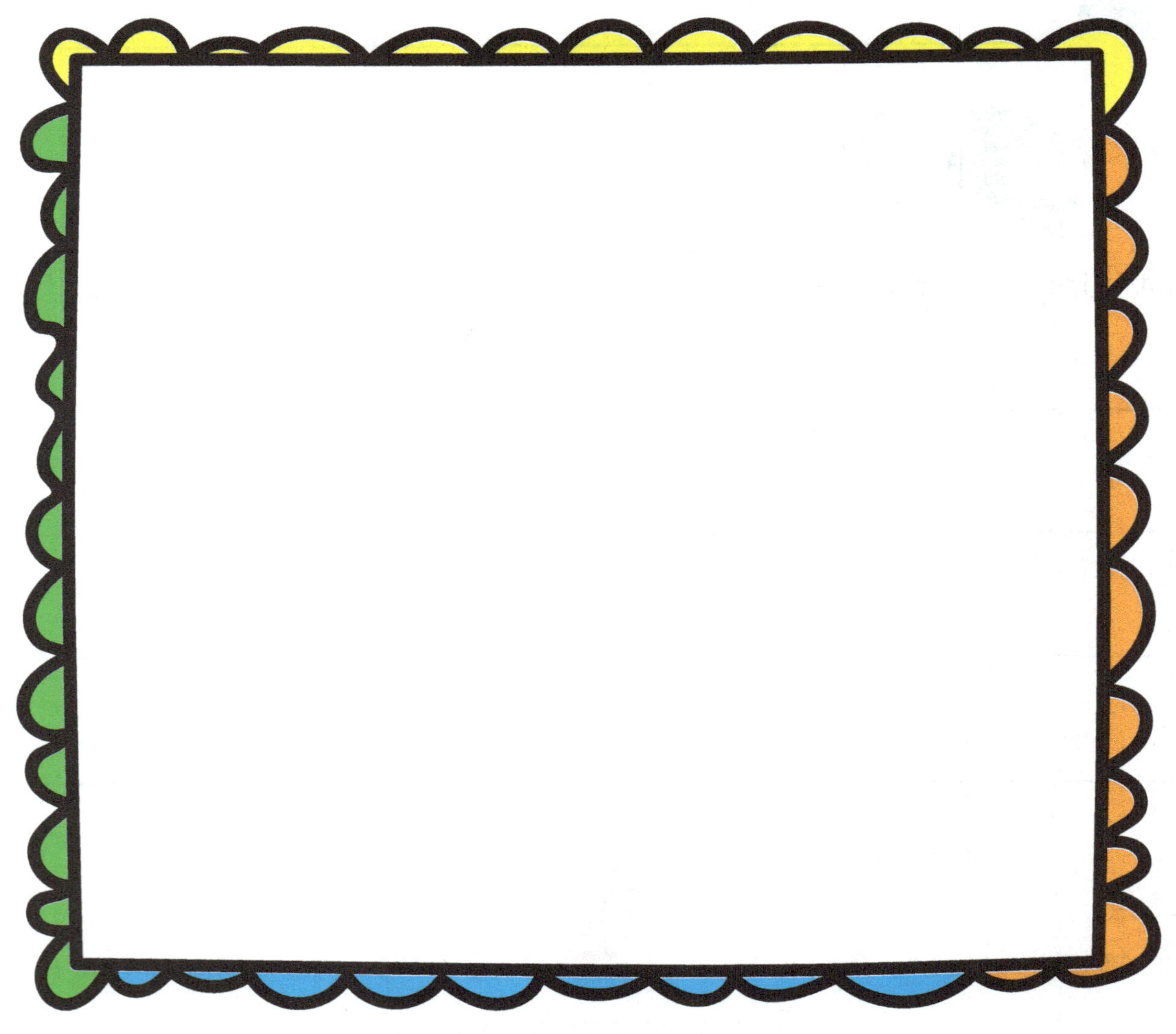

Describe your drawing: ______________________________

____

Glue or tape things from your trip here:

How did you get there?

☐ Car ☐ Boat ☐ Bus

☐ Airplane ☐ Camper ☐ Train

☐ Bicycle ☐ Walking ☐ Hot Air Balloon!

☐ Sunny

☐ Sun & Clouds

☐ Cloudy

☐ Rainy

☐ Snow

With whom did you go?

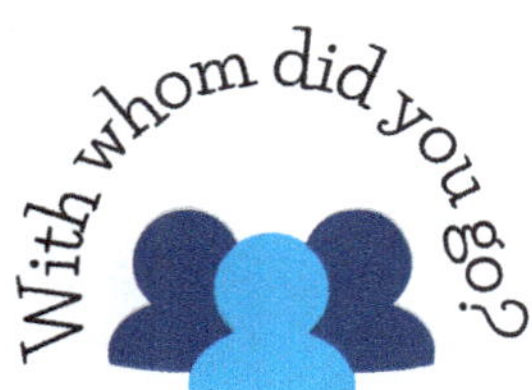

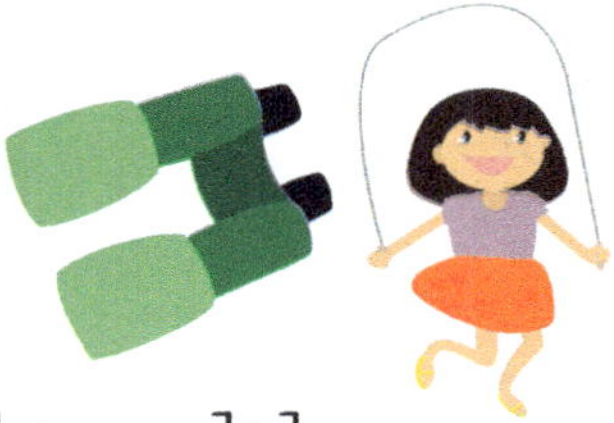

What things did you see or do?

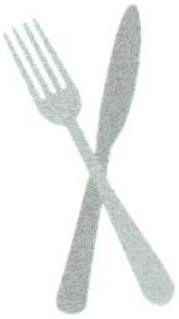

What did you eat?

What was your favorite part?

Draw a picture of something you saw:

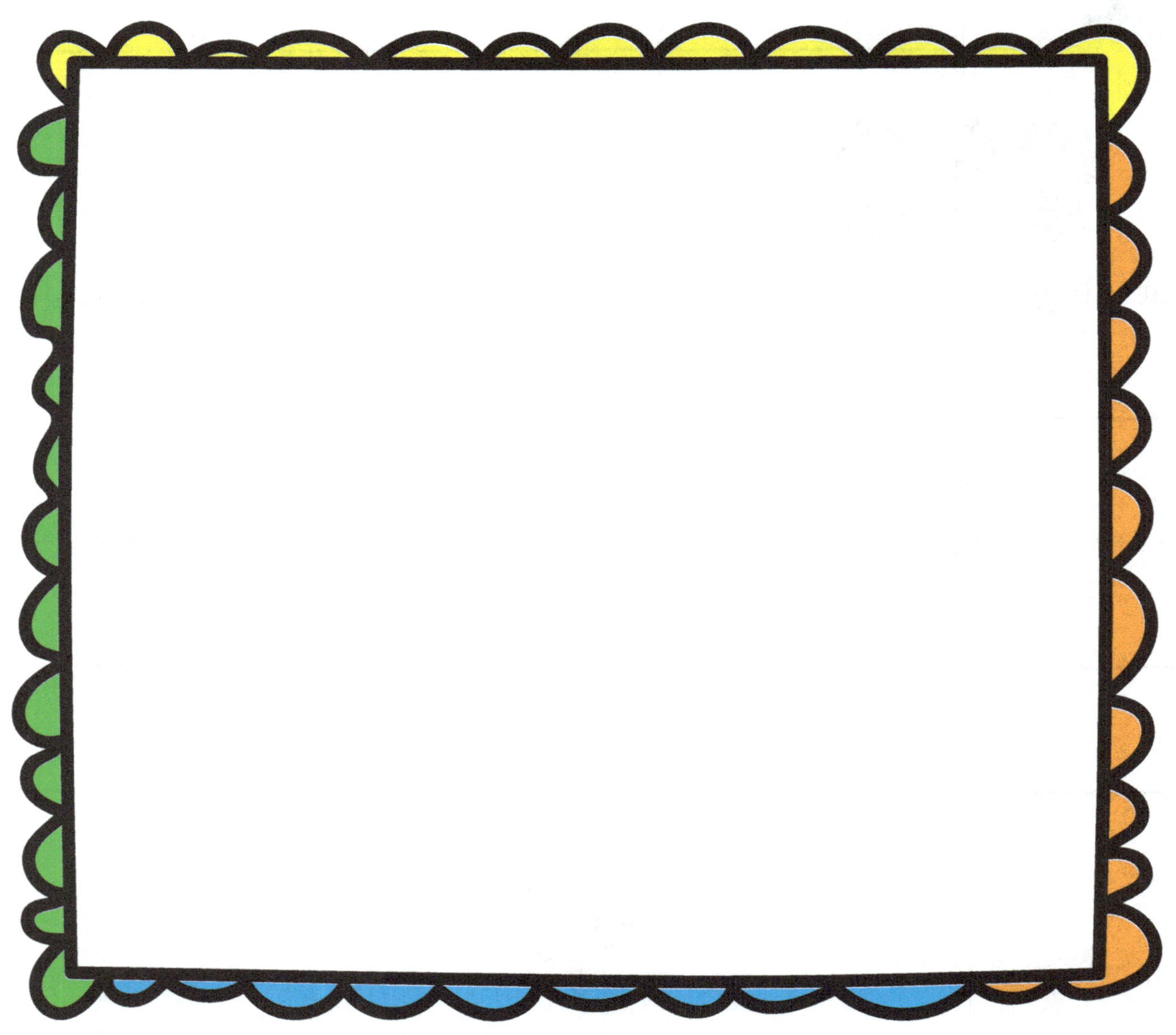

Describe your drawing: ______________________________

____

Glue or tape things from your trip here:

How did you get there?

- [ ] Car
- [ ] Boat
- [ ] Bus
- [ ] Airplane
- [ ] Camper
- [ ] Train
- [ ] Bicycle
- [ ] Walking
- [ ] Hot Air Balloon!

How was the weather?

- [ ] Sunny

- [ ] Sun & Clouds

- [ ] Cloudy

- [ ] Rainy

- [ ] Snow

What things did you see or do?

What did you eat?

What was your favorite part?

Draw a picture of something you saw:

Describe your drawing: ______________________________

____

Glue or tape things from your trip here:

How did you get there?

☐ Car ☐ Boat ☐ Bus

☐ Airplane ☐ Camper ☐ Train

☐ Bicycle ☐ Walking ☐ Hot Air Balloon!

☐ 

☐ 

☐ 

☐ 

☐ 

With whom did you go?

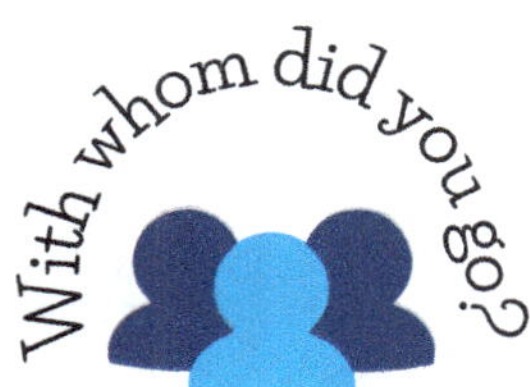

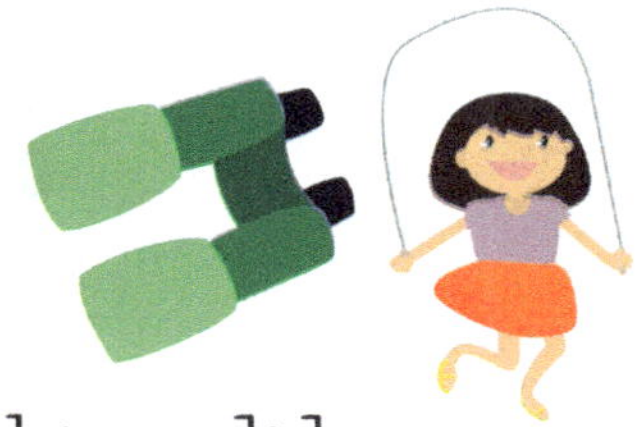

What things did you see or do?

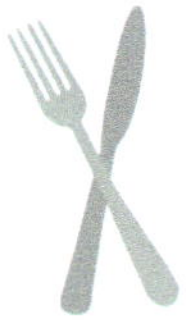

What did you eat?

What was your favorite part?

Draw a picture of something you saw:

Describe your drawing: ______________________________

____

Glue or tape things from your trip here:

How did you get there?

- [ ] Car
- [ ] Boat
- [ ] Bus
- [ ] Airplane
- [ ] Camper
- [ ] Train
- [ ] Bicycle
- [ ] Walking
- [ ] Hot Air Balloon!

- [ ] Sunny

- [ ] Sun & Clouds

- [ ] Cloudy

- [ ] Rainy

- [ ] Snow

With whom did you go?

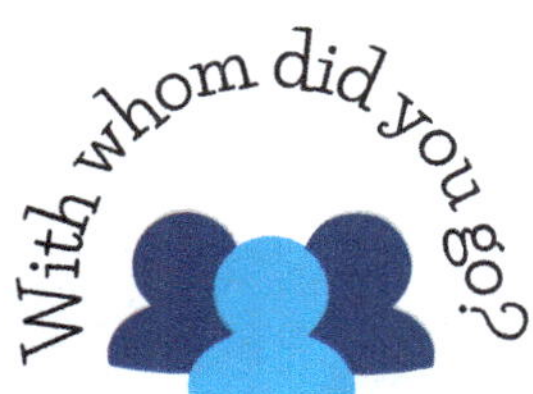

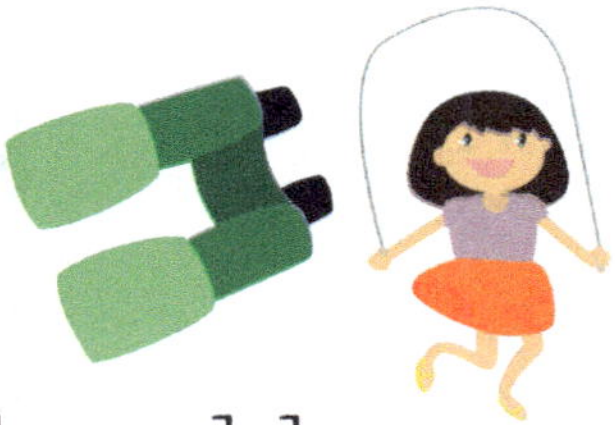

What things did you see or do?

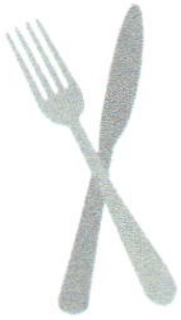

What did you eat?

What was your favorite part?

Draw a picture of something you saw:

Describe your drawing: ______________________________

____

Glue or tape things from your trip here:

When?

____

How did you get there?

☐ Car ☐ Boat ☐ Bus

☐ Airplane ☐ Camper ☐ Train

☐ Bicycle ☐ Walking ☐ Hot Air Balloon!

How was the weather?

☐ Sunny

☐ Sun & Clouds

☐ Cloudy

☐ Rainy

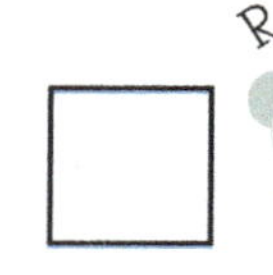

☐ Snow

What things did you see or do?

What did you eat?

What was your favorite part?

Draw a picture of something you saw:

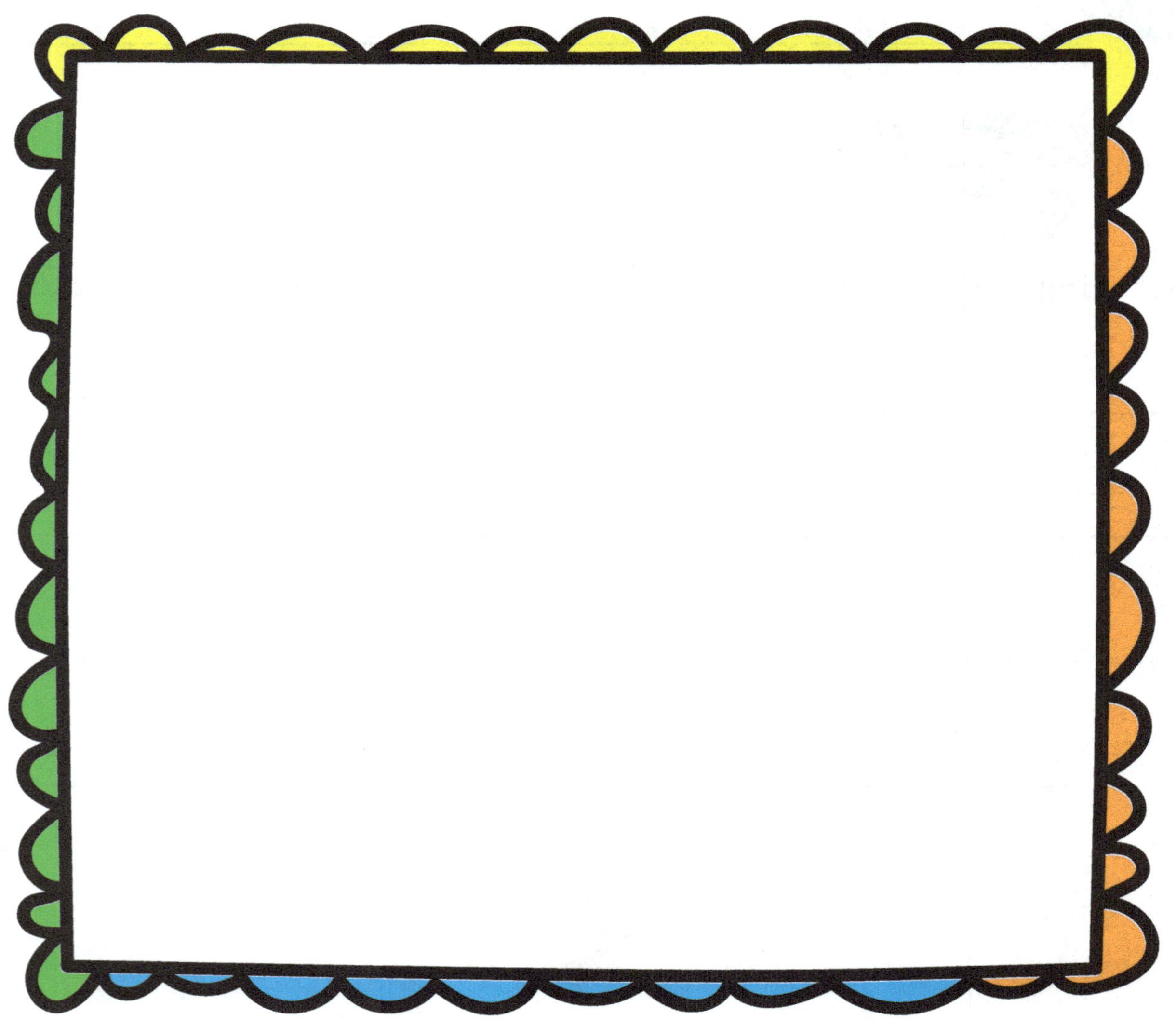

Describe your drawing: ____________________

____

Glue or tape things from your trip here:

How did you get there?

☐ Car

☐ Boat

☐ Bus

☐ Airplane

☐ Camper

☐ Train

☐ Bicycle

☐ Walking

☐ Hot Air Balloon!

☐ Sunny

☐ Sun & Clouds

☐ Cloudy

☐ Rainy

☐ Snow

With whom did you go?

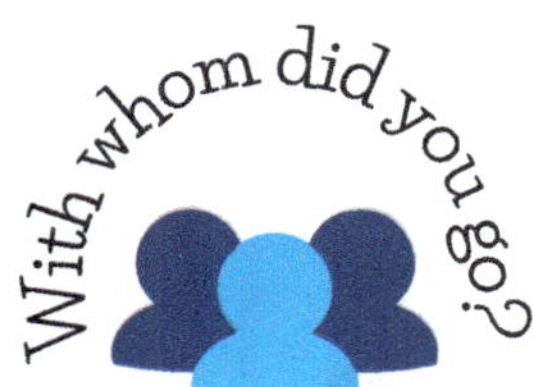

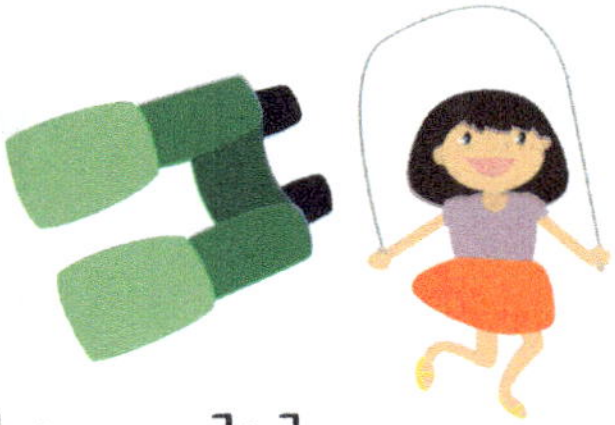

What things did you see or do?

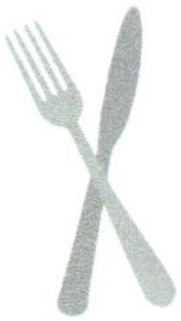

What did you eat?

What was your favorite part?

Draw a picture of something you saw:

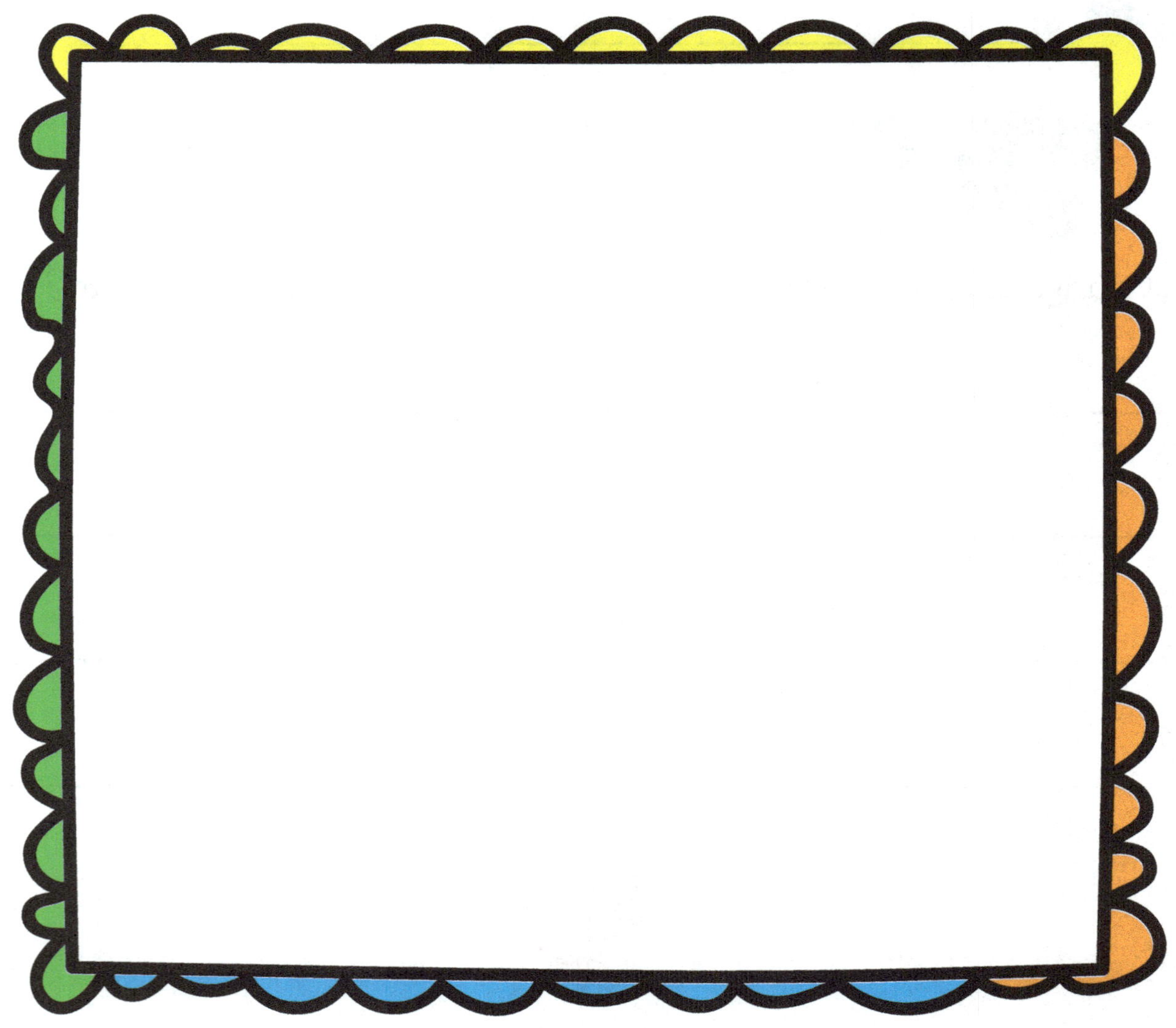

Describe your drawing: ______________________________

____

Glue or tape things from your trip here:

When?

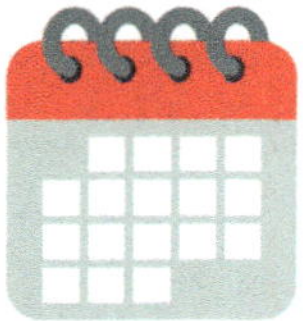

How did you get there?

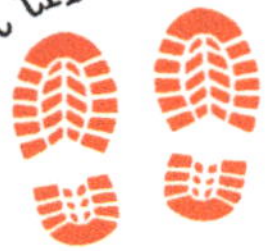

☐ Car 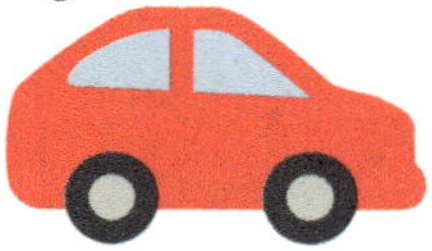 ☐ Boat 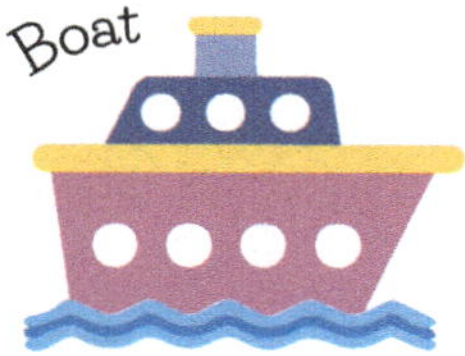 ☐ Bus

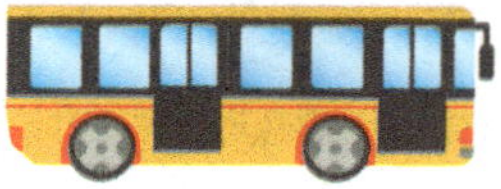

☐ Airplane 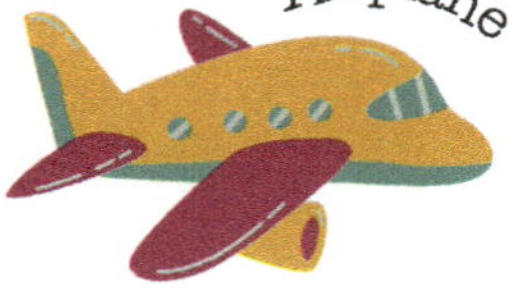 ☐ Camper 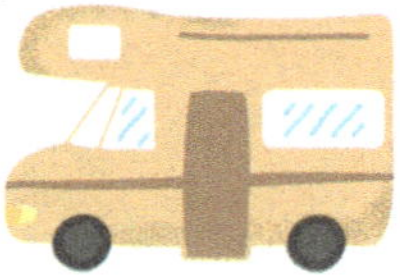 ☐ Train

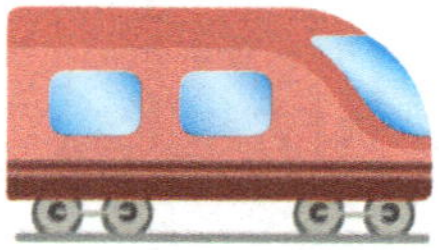

☐ Bicycle 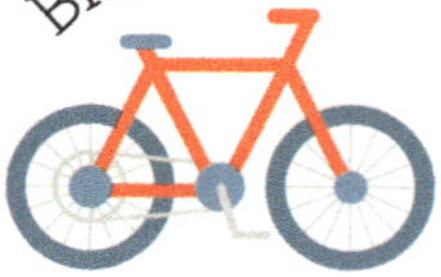 ☐ Walking 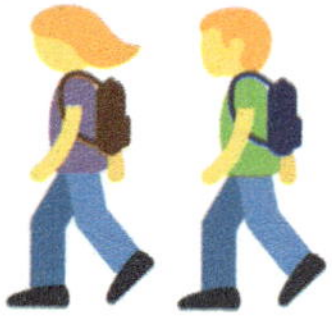 ☐ Hot Air Balloon!

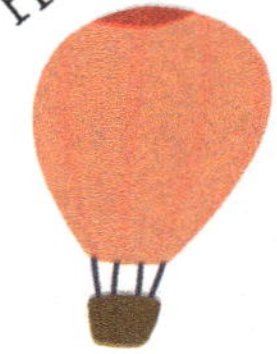

How was the weather?

☐ Sunny

☐ Sun & Clouds

☐ Cloudy

☐ Rainy

☐ Snow

What things did you see or do?

What did you eat?

What was your favorite part?

Draw a picture of something you saw:

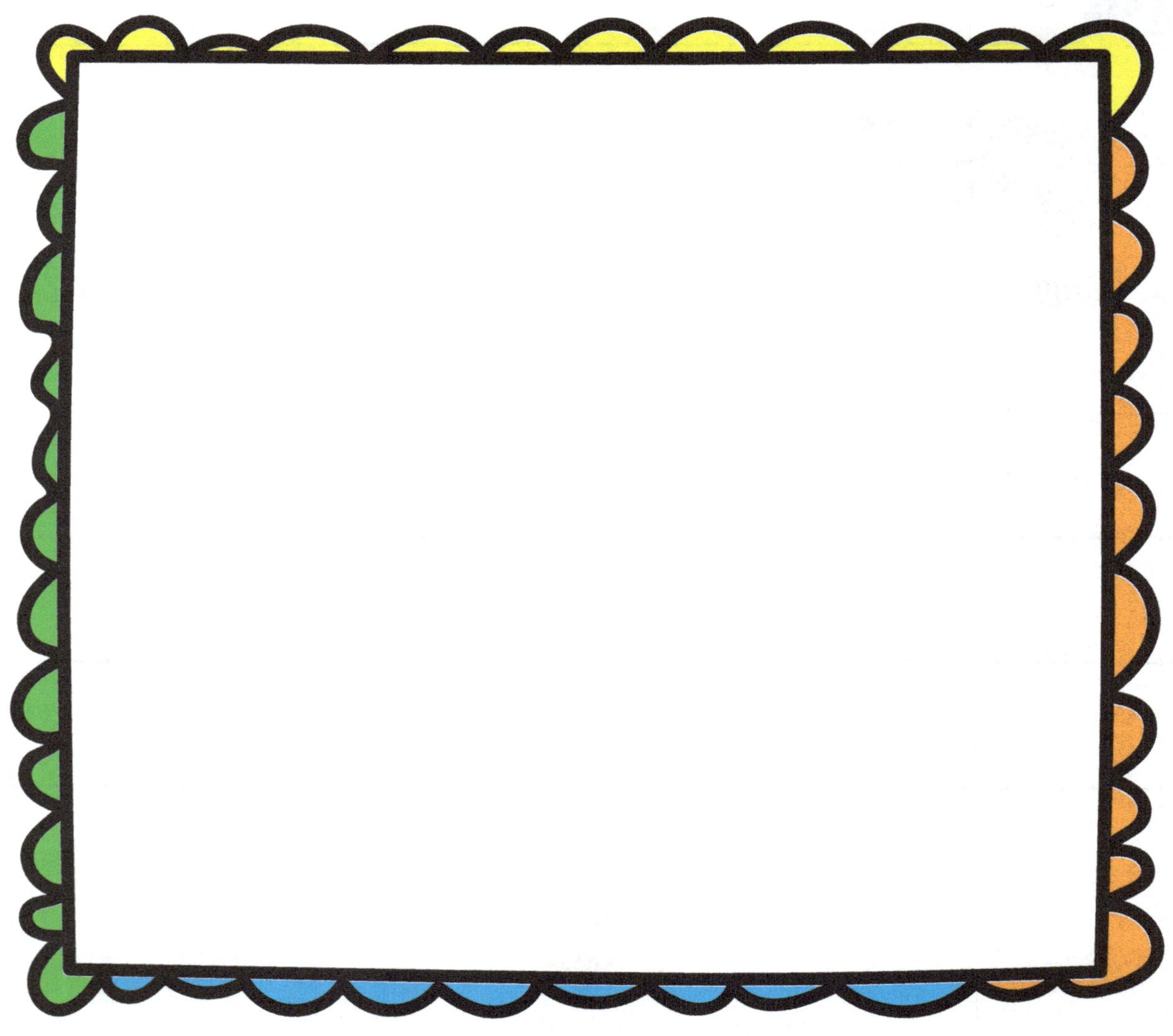

Describe your drawing: ______________________________

____

Glue or tape things from your trip here:

When?

How did you get there?

☐ Car

☐ Boat

☐ Bus

☐ Airplane

☐ Camper

☐ Train

☐ Bicycle

☐ Walking

☐ Hot Air Balloon!

How was the weather?

☐ Sunny

☐ Sun & Clouds

☐ Cloudy

☐ Rainy

☐ Snow

What things did you see or do?

What did you eat?

What was your favorite part?

Draw a picture of something you saw:

Describe your drawing: ______________________________

____

Glue or tape things from your trip here:

Travel Often

Create your own adventures

Create memories that last forever

Discover the books in the Kiba Tales series:

Find out more at
www.kibatales.com

About the Creator

Laura Hockensmith is the author of the Kiba Tales book series. She is also the author of 200+ whimsical poems on Instagram, starring the real-life Kiba.

Laura is an American, living in the Netherlands. She hopes to inspire children to travel and create their own adventures.

Made in the USA
Las Vegas, NV
01 November 2024